LIVING FROM THE
PRESENCE
LEADER'S GUIDE

LIVING FROM THE
PRESENCE
LEADER'S GUIDE

HEIDI BAKER
with ROLLAND BAKER

DESTINY IMAGE® PUBLISHERS, INC.

P.O. Box 310, Shippensburg, PA 17257-0310

"Promoting Inspired Lives."

This book and all other Destiny Image and Destiny Image Fiction books are available at Christian bookstores and distributors worldwide.

Cover design by Eileen Rockwell

Interior design by Terry Clifton

For more information on foreign distributors, call 717-532-3040.

Reach us on the Internet: www.destinyimage.com.

ISBN 13 TP: 978-0-7684-1238-3

ISBN eBook: 978-0-7684-4271-7

For Worldwide Distribution, Printed in the U.S.A.

1 2 3 4 5 6 7 8 / 21 20 19 18 17

CONTENTS

BASIC LEADER GUIDELINES

THIS STUDY IS DESIGNED TO HELP YOU DEVELOP A LIFESTYLE OF LIVING FROM the Presence of God under the active, continuous influence of the Spirit of God. What sets us apart as the people of God is the One who lives within us. The Christian life is not a journey of learning or doing; it's a lifelong, interactive relationship with One called God, the Holy Spirit. In the pages to come, prepare your heart to receive a reset. A walk with God is not about information or activity; it's about living from the Presence of the One who has made you His dwelling place! As such, this is an interactive study.

There are several different ways that you can engage this study. By no means is this forthcoming list comprehensive. Rather, these are the standard outlets recommended to facilitate this curriculum. We encourage you to seek the Lord's direction, be creative, and prepare for supernatural transformation in your Christian life.

When all is said and done, this curriculum is unique in that the end goal is *not* information—it is transformation. The sessions are intentionally sequenced to take every believer on a journey from information, to revelation, to transformation. Participants will receive a greater understanding of what partnership with Heaven looks like and learn how to practically live this supernatural lifestyle on a daily basis.

Here are some of the ways you can use the curriculum:

1. CHURCH SMALL GROUP

Often, churches feature a variety of different small group opportunities per season in terms of books, curriculum resources, and Bible studies. *Living from the Presence* would be included among the offerings for whatever season you are launching for the small group program.

It is recommended that you have at least four to five people to make up a small group and a maximum of twelve. If you end up with more than 12 members, either the group needs to multiply and break into two different groups or you should consider moving toward a church class model (which will be outlined below).

For a small group setting, here are the essentials:

- *Meeting place*: Either the leader's home or a space provided by the church.

- *Appropriate technology*: A DVD player attached to a TV that is large enough for all of the group members to see (and loud enough for everyone to hear).

- *Leader/Facilitator*: This person will often be the host, if the small group is being conducted at someone's home; but it can also be a team (husband/wife, two church leaders, etc.). The leader(s) will direct the session from beginning to end, from sending reminder e-mails to participating group members about the meetings, to closing out the sessions in prayer and dismissing everyone. That said, leaders might select certain people in the group to assist with various elements of the meeting—worship, prayer, ministry time, etc. A detailed description of what the group meetings should look like will follow in the pages to come.

Sample Schedule for Home Group Meeting (for a 7:00 P.M. meeting)

- Before arrival: Ensure that refreshments are ready by 6:15 P.M. If they need to be refrigerated, ensure they are preserved appropriately until 15 minutes prior to the official meeting time.

- 6:15 P.M.: Leaders arrive at meeting home or facility.

- 6:15–6:25 P.M.: Connect with hosts, co-hosts, and/or co-leaders to review the evening's program.

- 6:25–6:35 P.M.: Pray with hosts, co-hosts, and/or co-leaders for the evening's events. Here are some sample prayer directives:

  • For the Holy Spirit to move and minister freely.

  • For the teaching to connect with and transform all who hear it.

  • For dialogue and conversation that edifies.

- For comfort and transparency among group members.

- For the Presence of God to manifest during worship.

- For testimonies of answered prayers.

- For increased hunger for God's Presence and power.

■ 6:35–6:45 P.M.: Ensure technology is functioning properly!

- Test the DVDs featuring the teaching sessions, making sure they are set up to the appropriate session.

- If you are doing praise and worship, ensure that either the MP3 player or CD player is functional, set at an appropriate volume (not soft, but not incredibly loud), and that song sheets are available for everyone so they can sing along with the lyrics. (If you are tech savvy, you could do a PowerPoint or Keynote presentation featuring the lyrics.)

■ 6:45–7:00 P.M.: Welcome and greeting for guests.

■ 7:00–7:10 P.M.: Fellowship, community, and refreshments.

■ 7:10–7:12 P.M.: Gather everyone together in the meeting place.

■ 7:12–7:30 P.M.: Introductory prayer and worship.

■ 7:30–7:40 P.M.: Ministry and prayer time.

■ 7:40–8:00 P.M.: Watch DVD session.

■ 8:00–8:20 P.M.: Discuss DVD session.

■ 8:20–8:35 P.M.: Activation time.

■ 8:35–8:40 P.M.: Closing prayer and dismiss.

This sample schedule is *not* intended to lock you into a formula. It is simply provided as a template to help you get started. Our hope is that you customize it according to the unique needs of your group and sensitively navigate the activity of the Holy Spirit as He uses these sessions to supernaturally transform the lives of every person participating in the study.

2. SMALL GROUP CHURCH-WIDE CAMPAIGN

This would be the decision of the pastor or senior leadership of the church. In this model, the entire church would go through *Living from the Presence* in both the main services and ancillary small groups/life classes.

These campaigns would be marketed as *40 Days of Living from the Presence of God*. The pastor's weekend sermon would be based on the principles in *Living from the Presence*, and the Sunday school classes/life classes and/or small groups would also follow the *Living from the Presence* curriculum format.

3. CHURCH CLASS | MIDWEEK CLASS | SUNDAY SCHOOL CURRICULUM

Churches of all sizes offer a variety of classes purposed to develop members into more effective disciples of Jesus and agents of transformation in their spheres of influence.

Living from the Presence would be an invaluable addition to a church's class offering. Typically, churches offer a variety of topical classes targeted at men's needs, women's needs, marriage, family, finances, and various areas of Bible study.

Living from the Presence is a unique resource, as it does not fit in with the aforementioned traditional topics usually offered to the Church body. On the contrary, this study breaks down what it means to live from the presence of God under the active, continuous influence of the Spirit of God. While it may be difficult to facilitate dialogue in a class setting, it is certainly optional and recommended. The other way to successfully engage *Living from the Presence* in a class setting is to have a teacher/leader go through the questions/answers presented in the upcoming pages and use these as his or her teaching notes.

4. INDIVIDUAL STUDY

While the curriculum is designed for use in a group setting, it also works as a tool that can equip anyone who is looking to strengthen his or her spirit and soul.

Steps to Launching a *Living from the Presence* Group or Class

Prepare with Prayer!

Pray! If you are a **church leader**, prayerfully consider how *Living from the Presence* could transform the culture and climate of your church community! The Lord is raising up bodies of believers who bring transformation in their wake because of the overflow of a mind that's been reoriented to Heaven's perspective. Spend some time with the Holy Spirit, asking Him to give you vision for what this unique study will do for your church and, ultimately, how a Kingdom-minded people will transform your city and region.

If you are a **group leader** or **class facilitator**, pray for those who will be attending your group, signing up for your class, and will be positioning their lives to be transformed by the power and Presence of God in this study.

Prepare Practically!

Determine how you will be using the Living from the Presence curriculum.

Identify which of the following formats you will be using the curriculum in:

- Church-sponsored small group study

- Church-wide campaign

- Church class (Wednesday night, Sunday morning, etc.)

- Individual study

Determine a meeting location and ensure availability of appropriate equipment.

Keep in mind the number of people who may attend. You will also need AV (audio-visual) equipment. The more comfortable the setting, the more people will enjoy being there, and will spend more time ministering to each other!

A word of caution here: the larger the group, the greater the need for co-leaders or assistants. The ideal small group size is difficult to judge; however, once you get more than 10 to 12 people, it becomes difficult for each member to feel "heard." If your group is larger than 12 people, consider either having two or more small group discussion leaders or "multiplying" the larger group into two smaller ones.

Determine the format for your meetings.

The Presence of the Lord, which brings transformation, is cradled and stewarded well in the midst of organization. Structure should never replace spontaneity; on the contrary, having a plan and determining what type of format your meetings will take enables you to flow with the Holy Spirit and minister more effectively.

Also, by determining what kind of meeting you will be hosting, you are equipped to develop a schedule for the meeting, identify potential co-leaders, and order the appropriate number of resources.

Set a schedule for your meetings.

Once you have established the format for your meetings, set a schedule for your meetings. Some groups like to have a time of fellowship or socializing (either before or after the meeting begins) where light refreshments are offered. Some groups will want to incorporate times of worship and personal ministry into the small group or class. This is highly recommended for *Living from the Presence*, as the study is designed to be founded upon equipping and activating believers through encountering God's Presence. The video portion and discussion questions are intended to instruct believers, while the worship, times of ministry, group interaction, prayer time, and activation elements are purposed to engage them to live out what they just learned. *Living from the Presence* is not a lofty theological concept; it is a practical reality for every born-again believer. This study is intended to educate; but even more so, it is designed to activate believers and position them to steward their private, interior lives.

Establish a start date along with a weekly meeting day and time.

This eight-week curriculum should be followed consistently and consecutively. Be mindful of the fact that while there are eight weeks of material, most groups will want to meet one last time after completing the last week to celebrate, or designate their first meeting as a time to get to know each other and "break the ice." This is very normal and should be encouraged to continue the community momentum that the small group experience initiates. Typically, after the final session is completed, groups will often engage in a social activity—either going out to dinner together, seeing a movie, or something of the like.

Look far enough ahead on the calendar to account for anything that might interfere. Choose a day that works well for the members of your group. For a church class, be sure to coordinate the time with the appropriate ministry leader.

Advertise!

Getting the word out in multiple ways is most effective. Print out flyers, post a sign-up sheet, make an announcement in church services or group meetings, send out weekly e-mails and text messages, set up your own blog or website, or post the event on the social media avenue you and your group use most (Facebook, Twitter, etc.). A personal invitation or phone call is a great way to reach those who might need that little bit of extra encouragement to get involved.

For any type of small group or class to succeed, it must be endorsed by and encouraged from the leadership. For larger churches with multiple group/class offerings, it is wise to provide church members literature featuring all of the different small group/class options. This information should also be displayed online in an easily accessible page on your church website.

For smaller churches, it is a good idea for the pastor or a key leader to announce the launch of a small group course or class from the pulpit during an announcement time.

Gather your materials.

Each leader will need the *Living from the Presence* Leader's Kit, as well as the *Living from the Presence* DVD series.

Additionally, each participant will need a personal copy of the *Living from the Presence* interactive manual. It is recommended they also purchase the *Living from the Presence* DVD set for further enrichment and as a resource to complement their daily readings. However, they are able to engage in the exercises and participate in the group discussion apart from watching the videos.

We have found it best for the materials to all be purchased at one time—many booksellers and distributors offer discounts on multiple orders, and you are assured that each member will have their materials from the beginning of the course.

STEP FORWARD!

Arrive at your meeting in *plenty* of time to prepare; frazzled last-minute preparations do not put you in a place of "rest," and your group members will sense your stress! Ensure that all AV equipment is working properly and that you have ample supplies for each member. Nametags are a great idea, at least for the first couple of meetings. Icebreaker and introduction activities are also a good idea for the first meeting.

Pray for your members. As much as possible, make yourself available to them. As members increase in insight on strengthening themselves in the Lord, they will want to share that discovery! You will also need to encourage those who struggle, grow weary, or lose heart along the journey and through the process. Make sure your members stay committed so they experience the full benefits of this teaching.

Embrace the journey that you and your fellow members are embarking on to strengthen themselves in the Lord. Transformation begins within *you*!

Multiply yourself. Is there someone you know who was not able to attend your group? Help them to initiate their own small group now that you know how effective hosting *Living from the Presence* can be in a group setting!

THANK YOU

Thank you for embarking on a journey to equip the bride of Christ to be strong, peaceful, joyful, and who she is destined to be in this world.

LEADER CHECKLIST

ONE TO TWO MONTHS PRIOR

_____ Have you determined a start date for your class or small group?

_____ Have you determined the format, meeting day and time, and weekly meeting schedule?

_____ Have you selected a meeting location (making sure you have adequate space and AV equipment available)?

_____ Have you advertised? Do you have a sign-up sheet to ensure you order enough materials?

THREE WEEKS TO ONE MONTH PRIOR

_____ Have you ordered materials? You will need a copy of *Living from the Presence* Leader's Kit, along with copies of the workbook for each participant.

_____ Have you organized your meeting schedule/format?

ONE TO TWO WEEKS PRIOR

_____ Have you received all your materials?

_____ Have you reviewed the DVDs and your Leader's Kit to familiarize yourself with the material and to ensure everything is in order?

_____ Have you planned and organized the refreshments, if you are planning to provide them? Some leaders will handle this themselves, and some find it easier to allow participants to sign up to provide refreshments if they would like to do so.

_____ Have you advertised and promoted? This includes sending out e-mails to all participants, setting up a Facebook group, setting up a group through your church's database system (if available), promotion in the church bulletin, etc.

_____ Have you appointed co-leaders to assist you with the various portions of the group/class? While it is not necessary, it is helpful to have someone who is in charge of either leading (on guitar, keyboard, etc.) or arranging the worship music (putting songs on a CD, creating song lyric sheets, etc.). It is also helpful to have a prayer coordinator as well—someone who helps facilitate the prayer time, ensuring that all of the prayer needs are acknowledged and remembered, and assigning the various requests to group members who are willing to lift up those needs in prayer.

FIRST MEETING DAY

_____ Plan to arrive *early!* Give yourself extra time to set up the meeting space, double-check all AV equipment, and organize your materials. It might be helpful to ask participants to arrive 15 minutes early for the first meeting to allow for distribution of materials and any icebreaker activity you might have planned.

Session Discussion Questions:
WEEKLY OVERVIEW OF MEETINGS/GROUP SESSIONS

HERE ARE SOME INSTRUCTIONS ON HOW TO USE EACH OF THE WEEKLY Discussion Question guides.

WELCOME AND FELLOWSHIP TIME
(10–15 Minutes)

This usually begins five to ten minutes prior to the designated meeting time and typically continues up until ten minutes after the official starting time. Community is important. One of the issues in many small group/class environments is the lack of connectivity among the people. People walk around inspired and resourced, but they remain disconnected from other believers. Foster an environment where community is developed but, at the same time, not distracting. Distraction tends to be a problem that plagues small group settings more than classes.

Welcome: Greet everyone as they walk in. If it is a small group environment, as the host or leader, be intentional about connecting with each person as they enter the meeting space. If it is a church class environment, it is still recommended that the leader connect with each participant. However, there will be less pressure for the participants to feel connected immediately in a traditional class setting versus a more intimate small group environment.

Refreshments and materials: In the small group, you can serve refreshments and facilitate fellowship between group members. In a class setting, talk with the attendees and ensure that they purchase all of their necessary materials (workbook and optional copy of *Living from the Presence* DVD series). Ideally, the small group members will have received all of their resources prior to Week 1, but if not, ensure that the materials are present at the meeting and available for group members to pick up or purchase. It is advisable that you have several copies of the workbook and book available at the small group meeting, just in case people did not receive their copies at the designated time.

Call the meeting to order: This involves gathering everyone together in the appropriate place and clearly announcing that the meeting is getting ready to start.

Pray! Open every session in prayer, specifically addressing the topic that you will be covering in the upcoming meeting time. Invite the Presence of the Holy Spirit to come, move among the group members, minister to them individually, reveal Jesus, and stir greater hunger in each participant to experience *more* of God's power in their lives.

INTRODUCTIONS
(10 Minutes—First Class Only)

While a time of formal introduction should only be done on the first week of the class/session, it is recommended that in subsequent meetings group members state their names when addressing a question, making a prayer request, giving a comment, etc., just to ensure everyone is familiar with names. You are also welcome to do a short icebreaker activity at this time.

Introduce yourself and allow each participant to briefly introduce him/herself. This should work fine for both small group and class environments. In a small group, you can go around the room and have each person introduce himself/herself one at a time. In a classroom setting, establish some type of flow and then have each person give a quick introduction (name, interesting factoid, etc.).

Discuss the schedule for the meetings. Provide participants an overview of what the next eight weeks will look like. If you plan to do any social activities, you might want to advertise this right up front, noting that while the curriculum runs for eight weeks, there will be a ninth session dedicated to fellowship and some type of fun activity.

Distribute materials to each participant. Briefly orient the participants to the book and workbook, explaining the 10–15 minute time commitment for every day (Monday through Friday). Encourage each person to engage fully in this journey—they will get out of it only as much as they invest. The purpose for the daily reinforcement activities is *not* to add busywork to their lives. This is actually a way to cultivate a habit of Bible study and daily time renewing their minds, starting with just 10–15 minutes a day. Morning, evening, afternoon—*when* does not matter. The key is making the decision to engage.

WORSHIP
(15 Minutes—Optional for the First Meeting)

Fifteen minutes is a solid time for a worship segment. That said, it all depends upon the culture of your group. If everyone is okay with doing 30 minutes of praise and worship, by all means, go for it!

For this particular curriculum, a worship segment is highly recommended, as true and lasting transformation happens as we continually encounter God's Presence.

If a group chooses to do a worship segment, usually they decide to begin on the second week. It often takes an introductory meeting for everyone to become acquainted with one another, and comfortable with their surroundings before they open up together in worship.

On the other hand, if the group members are already comfortable with one another and they are ready to launch immediately into a time of worship, they should definitely begin on the first meeting.

While it has been unusual for Sunday school/church classes to have a time of worship during their sessions, it is actually a powerful way to prepare participants to receive the truth being shared in the *Living from the Presence* sessions. In addition, pre-service worship (if the class is being held prior to a Sunday morning worship experience) actually stirs hunger in the participants for greater encounters with God's Presence, both corporately and congregationally.

If the class is held midweek (or on a day where there is *no* church service going on), a praise and worship component is a wonderful way to refresh believers in God's Presence as they are given the privilege of coming together, midweek, and corporately experiencing His Presence.

PRAYER/MINISTRY TIME
(5–15 Minutes)

At this point, you will transition from either welcome or worship into a time of prayer.

Just like praise and worship, it is recommended that this initial time of prayer be five to ten minutes in length; but if the group is made up of people who do not mind praying longer, it should not be discouraged. The key is stewarding everyone's time well while maintaining focus on the most important things at hand.

Prayer should be navigated carefully, as there will always be people who use it as an opportunity to speak longer than necessary, vent about the circumstances in their lives, or potentially gossip about other people.

At the same time, there are real people carrying deep needs to the group and they need supernatural ministry. The prayer component is a time where group members will not just receive prayer, but also learn how to exercise Jesus' authority in their own lives and witness breakthrough in their circumstances.

This prayer time doubles as a ministry time, where believers are encouraged to flow in the gifts of the Holy Spirit. After the door is opened through worship, the atmosphere is typically charged with God's Presence. It is quite common for people to receive words of knowledge, words of wisdom, prophetic words, and for other manifestations of the Holy Spirit to take place in these times (see 1 Cor. 12). This is a safe environment for people to "practice" these gifts, take risks, etc. However, if there are individuals who demonstrate consistent disorder, are unceasingly distracting, have problems/issues that move beyond the scope of this particular curriculum (and appear to need specialized counseling), or have issues that veer more into the theological realm, it is best for you to refer these individuals to an appropriate leader in the church who can address these particular issues privately.

If you are such a leader, you can either point them to a different person, or you can encourage them to save their questions/comments and you will address them outside of the group context, as you do not want to distract from what God is doing in these vital moments together.

TRANSITION TIME

At this point, you will transition from prayer/ministry time to watching the *Living from the Presence* DVDs.

Group leaders/class teachers: It is recommended that you have the DVD in the player and are all ready to press "play" on the appropriate session.

VIDEO/TEACHING
(20–25 Minutes)

During this time, group members will fill in the blanks in their participant workbooks. All of the information they need to complete this assignment will appear on screen during the session. However, there will be additional information that appears on screen that will *not* go in the "fill in the blank" section. This is simply for the viewer's own notation.

SCRIPTURE

We have selected a Scripture passage that accompanies the theme for the week. You or someone else can read this out loud.

SUMMARY

There is also short summary of the week's topic before the discussion questions. You can read this prior to the group meeting to provide you with a summary of that week's session.

INTERACTIVE QUESTIONS
(20–30 Minutes)

In the Leader's Guide there will be a number of questions to ask the group, most of which are in the workbook also. Some questions will be phrased so you can ask them directly, others may have instructions or suggestions for how you can guide the discussion. The sentences in bold are directions for you.

Some lessons will have more questions than others. Also, there might be some instances where you choose to cut out certain questions for the sake of time. This is entirely up to you, and in a circumstance where the Holy Spirit is moving and appears to be highlighting some questions more than others, flow in sync with the Holy Spirit. He will not steer you wrong!

Some of the questions will lead with a Scripture verse. To engage group members, you can ask for volunteers to read the Scripture verse(s). As you ask the question in the group setting, encourage more than one person to provide an answer. Usually, you will have some people who are way off in their responses, but you will also have those who provide *part* of the correct answer.

There is a very intentional flow in the order of questions. The questions will usually start out by addressing a problem, misconception, or false understanding, and are designed to take participants to a point of strategically addressing the problem, and then taking appropriate action.

The problem with many curriculum studies is in the question/answer section. Participants may feel like the conversation was lively, the dialogue insightful, and that the meeting was an overall success; but when all is said and done, the question, *"What do I do next?"* is not sufficiently answered.

This is why every discussion time will be followed with an activation segment.

ACTIVATION
(5–10 Minutes)

- Each activation segment should be five to ten minutes at the *minimum*, as this is the place where believers begin putting action to what they just learned.

- The activation segment will be custom-tailored for the session covered.

- Even though every group member might not be able to participate in the activation exercise, it gives them a visual for what it looks like to demonstrate the concept that they just studied.

GOAL

After the activation exercise, we have included a brief summary of the "goal" from that unique session. This is what participants should walk away from each session knowing and applying.

PLANS FOR THE NEXT WEEK
(2 Minutes)

Remind group members about daily exercises in the workbook. Encourage everyone to participate fully in this journey in order to get the most out of it. The daily exercises should not take more than 15–20 minutes and they will make an ideal 40-day themed Bible study.

Be sure to let group members know if the meeting location will change or differ from week to week, or if there are any other relevant announcements to your group/class. Weekly e-mails, Facebook updates, and text messages are great tools to communicate with your group. If your church has a database tool that allows for communication between small group/class leaders and members, that is an effective avenue for interaction as well.

CLOSE IN PRAYER

This is a good opportunity to ask for a volunteer to conclude the meeting with prayer.

Week

1

BUILDING YOUR THEOLOGY OF GOD'S PRESENCE

Rolland Baker

PRAYER FOCUS: ASK THE LORD TO HELP EVERY PARTICIPANT 1) UNDERSTAND THE importance of establishing a solid theological foundation for who God is and 2) learn how to build their life upon the truth of His identity.

FELLOWSHIP, WELCOME, AND INTRODUCTIONS
(20-30 Minutes—For the First Meeting)

Welcome everyone as they walk in. If it is a small group environment, as the host or leader, be intentional about connecting with each person as they come to the meeting space. If it is a church class environment, it is still recommended that the leader connects with each participant. However, there will be less pressure for the participants to feel connected immediately in a traditional class setting versus a more intimate small group environment.

In the small group, serve refreshments and facilitate fellowship between group members. In a class setting, talk with the attendees and ensure that they receive all of their necessary materials (the workbook and a copy of *Living from the Presence DVD series if they have ordered it*).

Introduce yourself and allow participants to briefly introduce themselves as well. This should work fine for both small group and class environments. In a small group, you can go around the room and have each person introduce him or herself, one at a time. In a classroom setting, establish some type of flow and then have each person give a quick introduction (name, interesting factoid, etc.).

Discuss the schedule for the meetings. Provide participants an overview of what the next eight weeks will look like. If you plan to do any type of social activity, you might want to advertise this at the start, noting that while the curriculum runs for eight weeks, there will be a ninth meeting dedicated to fellowship and some type of fun activity. However, you might come up with this idea later on in the actual study.

Distribute materials to each participant. Briefly orient the participants to the workbook, explaining the 15–20 minute time commitment for each day. Encourage each person to engage fully in this journey—they will get out of it only as much as they invest. The purpose for the daily reinforcement activities is *not* to add busywork to their lives. This is actually a way to cultivate a habit of Bible study and daily time pursuing God's Presence, starting with just 15–20 minutes. Morning, evening, afternoon—*when* does not matter. The key is making the decision to engage.

OPENING PRAYER

WORSHIP
(15 Minutes—Optional for First Meeting)

If a group chooses to do a worship segment, often they decide to begin on the second week. It usually takes an introductory meeting for everyone to become acquainted with one another and comfortable with their surroundings before they open up in worship.

On the other hand, if the group members are already comfortable with one another and they are ready to launch right into a time of worship, they should definitely go for it!

PRAYER/MINISTRY TIME
(5–15 Minutes)

VIDEO/TEACHING
(20 Minutes)

SCRIPTURE

For by him all things were created, in heaven and on earth, visible and invisible, whether thrones or dominions or rulers or authorities—all things were created through him and for him (Colossians 1:16 ESV).

SUMMARY

It's important for you to understand that the Presence of God is not a thing; it's not an additional member of the Trinity—Father, Son, Spirit, and Presence. The Presence of God is a Person, and in order for you to experience His Presence in the measure that's available, it's important for you to establish a solid theological foundation for *who* God is.

Even though more learning is not the key to a life saturated in the Presence of God, there are certain truths we need to build our lives upon. Truth is the gateway to experience. Before you can pursue Bible experience, you need to first have a foundation of Bible truth, for Bible truth is what establishes your appetite for Bible experience.

There are many in the body of Christ, particularly in Spirit-empowered circles, who passionately pursue experience, and rightly so. Then, there are streams and denominations that uphold the supremacy of God's written Word, *truth*. They are equally as correct. The problem is when truth and experience exist separated from one another. This produces cultures where people become puffed up with knowledge (all *truth*) or people move beyond Bible parameters and pursue experiences that are not the will of God (all *experience*).

To fully experience God, it's best to start with a foundation of truth. Then, based on the parameters of that truth, you can press in to actually experience the reality that truth claims is available.

INTERACTIVE QUESTIONS
(25–30 Minutes)

1. What does "freedom in the house" look like? How do you understand *yourself* to be the "house" of God?

2. Discuss: Why do you think it's important to have a correct theology of God?

3. How does your theology and understanding of who God is actually determine what you experience of His Presence?

4. Read Proverbs 9:10. How is the *fear of the Lord* connected with how we experience His Presence? Explain your understanding of what the fear of the Lord is and how it's so beneficial.

   The fear of the Lord is the beginning of wisdom, and knowledge of the Holy One is understanding.

5. What does salvation mean to you? What do you think it means to different people? Why do you think it's important to know what Jesus saved you from?

6. What does the following statement mean to you: "*God is in control*"? How does your view of God being in control positively impact your life and walk with the Lord?

7. Discuss the following statement: "When God moved in, Heaven began" (based on John 17:3).

   Now this is eternal life: that they know you, the only true God, and Jesus Christ, whom you have sent.

ACTIVATION EXERCISE

Meditate on the truth that *you* are the temple of God. You are the house of the Holy Spirit! In whatever context you have available to you, put this truth into practice.

Group Activation

Encourage each participant to focus on the Person and Presence of the Spirit dwelling within them. If need be, create an atmosphere of quiet reflection and soft worship—if possible. Sometimes, we allow worship to distract us from the fact that God lives within us.

Individual Activation

Focus inward—not on yourself, but on Christ in you. "Christ in you" is possible because the Holy Spirit has made you His home, His preferred dwelling place. Ask God to increase your awareness of the closeness of His Presence. Even though Heaven is your destination one day, Heaven can also be your experience *today* through the abiding Presence of the Spirit.

PLANS FOR THE NEXT WEEK
(2 Minutes)

Point out Day 1 through Day 5 in the workbook. Encourage everyone to participate fully in this daily journey in order to get the most out of it.

CLOSE IN PRAYER

Week
1

Video Listening Guide:
BUILDING YOUR THEOLOGY
OF GOD'S PRESENCE

Rolland Baker

BEFORE YOU CAN PURSUE BIBLE EXPERIENCE, YOU NEED TO FIRST HAVE A foundation of Bible truth, for Bible truth is what establishes your appetite for Bible experience.

To fully experience God, it's best to start with a foundation of truth. Then, based on the parameters of that truth, you can press in to actually experience the reality that truth claims is available.

HOW TO BUILD YOUR THEOLOGY OF GOD'S PRESENCE

1. Establish a relationship with God marked by the freedom He offers by understanding that wherever His Spirit is present, so is His freedom.

2. Understand God's nature—the aspects of His character—in order to draw close to Him.

3. Receive the grace of God given to us in Jesus even as you embrace a fear of the Lord that leads to knowledge and wisdom, awe, reverence, respect, and honor.

4. Know that God is sovereign and in control. He is the great "I Am."

5. Embrace the life message of Jesus Christ in your heart and receive a Kingdom not made with human hands.

DELIGHTING IN HIS MIRACLE-WORKING PRESENCE

Rolland Baker

PRAYER FOCUS: ASK THE LORD TO HELP EVERY PARTICIPANT QUIET THEIR MIND and their spirit as they allow the Lord to invite them into His presence.

FELLOWSHIP AND WELCOME
(15–20 Minutes)

Welcome everyone as they walk in. Be sure to identify any new members who were not at the previous session, have them introduce themselves so everyone is acquainted, and be sure that they receive the appropriate materials—workbook and book.

In the small group, **serve refreshments and facilitate fellowship** between group members. In a class setting, talk with the attendees—ask how their week has been and maintain a focus on what God *has done* and *is doing*.

Encourage everyone to gather in the meeting place. If it is a classroom setting, make an announcement that it is time to sit down and begin the session. If it is a small group, ensure everyone makes their way to the designated meeting space.

OPENING PRAYER

WORSHIP
(15–20 Minutes)

When it comes to the worship element, it can be executed in both small group and church class settings. While a worship time is not mandatory, it is highly encouraged, as the fundamental goal of this curriculum is to foster each participant's increased understanding and outworking of the supernatural realm. This is where true, lasting transformation takes place. Worship is a wonderful way of opening each session and setting everyone's perspective on what the class is about—not accumulating more information, but pursuing the One who is at the center of it all.

PRAYER/MINISTRY TIME
(5–15 Minutes)

VIDEO/TEACHING
(20 Minutes)

SCRIPTURE

With your hand of love is upon my life, you impart a Father's blessing to me. This is just too wonderful, deep, and incomprehensible! ...Wherever I go, your hand will guide me; your strength will empower me. It's impossible to disappear from you or to ask the darkness to hide me; for your presence is everywhere bringing light into my night! There is no such thing as darkness with you. The night, to you, is as bright as the day (Psalms 139:5-6,10-12 TPT).

SUMMARY

The joy of the Lord is a gift that flows from intimacy with the Giver. Joy is a fruit of the Spirit and the outcome of the Christian life; it is what you get when you get Jesus. His very Presence brings delight (see John 15:11). As we live in His glorious Presence, joy will bubble out of us in an unprecedented manner until it becomes a river gushing from the rushing waters of His love. Our delight in God is a natural reaction to His Presence and an expression of His Kingdom. It is our strength (see Neh. 8:10). Make no mistake about it—when you experience the joy down in your heart, you will be excited about sharing it with whomever you meet. As His love flows from you, you will find yourself longing desperately to go to the lost and broken with His miracle-working Presence. God is calling out to you every day, inviting you into His Presence. If you wait there with Him, when the time is right He will send you out. And when you go, you will mount up on wings of eagles, soaring with Him. God is calling you to live your life in intimacy with Jesus, fearlessly and passionately manifesting His glory, producing fruit in every season.

Jesus is a priceless lover, and it will cost you everything to love Him, but oh the joy you will receive in return! Fall into His arms today. Delight in His Presence.

INTERACTIVE QUESTIONS
(25–30 Minutes)

1. What is *your* natural reaction to the Presence of God?

2. Discuss: How is your reaction an expression of His Kingdom?

3. How is God daily inviting you into His Presence? What does His invitation look like for you? Describe your response to His invitation.

4. Read First Peter 1:13–16. "*For it is written: 'Be holy, because I am holy'*" (1 Pet. 1:16). Explain your understanding of what it means to be holy. How can we become holy?

5. Based on Psalm 1 and other Scriptures, what does it means to bear fruit in every season?

   What delight comes to those who follow God's ways! …Bearing fruit in every season of their lives. They are never dry, never fainting, ever blessed, ever prosperous (Psalm 1:1,3 TPT).

6. How do you describe intimacy with the Lord?

_____

_____

_____

_____

After people share their natural reactions to the Presence of God, transition immediately to the *Activation Exercise*. The goal of having people share testimonies of their reactions to God's Presence is to strengthen faith to engage the activation exercise.

ACTIVATION: EXPERIENCING GOD IN AN INTIMATE WAY

Meditate on the truth that the joy of the Lord is your strength. He is your glory-song!

Take time now to come into His Presence.

Group Activation

Allow each person to draw away from any distractions and get alone with God in an atmosphere conducive to listening and reflection. When you come back together, invite those who feel led to share their meditations. Once the time of sharing is finished, consider joining together for a few minutes of joyous spontaneous worship.

Individual Activation

Eliminate distractions. Find a quiet place where you can be totally alone. Allow the Lord to invite you into His Presence. Ask Him to fill you with His joy. As His joy comes upon you, allow yourself to express this joy. Sing, dance, laugh with Him! Let yourself be overcome as you delight in His Presence.

Goal: To train participants to encounter the Presence of God in an intimate way.

PLANS FOR THE NEXT WEEK
(2 Minutes)

Encourage group members to stay up to date with their daily exercises in the *Living from the Presence Interactive Manual.*

CLOSE IN PRAYER

Week

2

Video Listening Guide:
DELIGHTING IN HIS MIRACLE-WORKING PRESENCE

Rolland Baker

TO LIVE UNDER THE ACTIVE, CONTINUOUS INFLUENCE OF THE SPIRIT OF GOD with great joy is a gift that flows from intimacy with the Giver.

Joy is a fruit of the Spirit and the outcome of the Christian life; it is what you get when you get Jesus.

HOW TO DELIGHT IN HIS MIRACLE-WORKING PRESENCE

1. To be marked by joy: God is inviting you into His Presence daily. Are you responding positively to His invitation?

2. To be holy: God calls us to come out and be separate, to be holy, set apart from the profane, dedicating ourselves to the things of God.

3. To know Christ intimately: Consider everything a loss in view of the surpassing value of knowing Christ Jesus.

4. To be an expression of His Kingdom: The reign of God is manifested first in our hearts as righteousness, peace, and joy that translate into His love that overflows our lives.

5. To bear fruit in every season: As His Presence reigns and rains in our hearts, it fills us with the knowledge of God's will in the power of His Holy Spirit, releasing fruit for the Kingdom.

3

FINDING THE PERSON
BEHIND THE PRESENCE

Rolland Baker

PRAYER FOCUS: ASK THE LORD TO HELP EVERY PARTICIPANT PRESS IN TO discover the person of God behind His Presence.

FELLOWSHIP AND WELCOME
(10–15 Minutes)

Welcome everyone as they walk in. Be sure to identify any new members who were not at the previous session, and be sure that they receive the appropriate materials—workbook and book.

Encourage everyone to congregate in the meeting place. If it is a classroom setting, make an announcement that it is time to sit down and begin the session. If it is a small group, ensure everyone makes their way to the designated meeting space.

OPENING PRAYER

WORSHIP
(15–20 Minutes)

PRAYER/MINISTRY TIME
(5–15 Minutes)

VIDEO/TEACHING
(20 Minutes)

SCRIPTURE

"Let not the wise boast of their wisdom or the strong boast of their strength or the rich boast of their riches, but let the one who boasts boast about this: that they have the understanding to know me, that I am the Lord, who exercises kindness, justice and righteousness on earth, for in these I delight," declares the Lord (Jeremiah 9:23-24).

SUMMARY

From being *in* His presence, we can live *from* His presence—going *out* of the house, *out* of the church, *out* of Bible studies and going *into* the marketplace, the workplace, the mission fields, the hospitals, the retirement centers, and every place God urges us to go.

As we discover the Person of Jesus behind His Presence, the legalism of religion gives way to the freedom of walking in holiness. Some think that holiness means you have to stash yourself away from life lest its temptations lure you into unholy living. Actually, quite the opposite is true. When you find the Person behind the Presence, you become so full that it is impossible to keep to yourself. You become so full of Him that fleshly things hold no sway with you. When you experience His Presence in the secret place, it will naturally burst forth from you into your everyday reality. You won't just go forth, you'll *run* forth into the world full of passion to share the Good News because it will be impossible to keep it to yourself.

INTERACTIVE QUESTIONS
(25–30 Minutes)

1. The beloved disciple John found his identity not in knowing Jesus but in Jesus's love. How would you go about following John's example to the heart of Jesus?

2. What does it look like to live out your relationship with God from a place of Presence?

3. Explain the upside-down nature of the Kingdom of God as Jesus explained it in the Gospel of Matthew. Give three examples.

4. Describe how you faithfully represent Jesus' upside-down Kingdom?

5. How would you define God's sovereignty? What does it mean to honor God's sovereignty?

6. In light of Paul's prayer for the Ephesians, how are we made complete in God?

7. Describe what it looks like to "find Jesus."

ACTIVATION: LEARNING TO LIVE WITH A GREATER LEVEL OF TRUST IN GOD

Read Daniel 6:10–23 and Romans 15:13.

According to Romans 15:13, where does our hope come from? How is our hope related to our level of trust? Explain your answers from a New Covenant perspective versus the Old Covenant.

Do you just want a relationship Jesus that is sweet and comforting, or are you willing to trust Him even when it means turning your life upside down?

Group Activation

Give group members time to reflect on the scriptures and questions in the Activation Exercise, and then ask them to share their answers with a willingness to be vulnerable.

Individual Activation

Think on your level of trust in God, reflecting on how vulnerable you feel at the prospect of trusting Him to the point of turning your life upside down. Explain how your trust is based on either Old Covenant thinking or New Covenant.

PLANS FOR THE NEXT WEEK
(2 Minutes)

Encourage group members to stay up to date with their daily exercises in the *Living from the Presence Interactive Manual.*

CLOSE IN PRAYER

Week

3

Video Listening Guide:
FINDING THE PERSON
BEHIND THE PRESENCE

Rolland Baker

WHEN YOU EXPERIENCE HIS PRESENCE IN THE SECRET PLACE, IT WILL NATURALLY burst forth from you into your everyday reality.

You won't just go forth, you'll *run* forth into the world full of passion to share the Good News because it will be impossible to keep it to yourself.

HOW TO FIND THE PERSON BEHIND THE PRESENCE

1. Learn to distinguish between God's presents and His Presence. Fall in love with the One from whose Presence you are living.

2. Find Jesus! He is the prefect lover who will transform your heart into what it was designed for.

3. Seek the purity and simplicity of devotion to Christ above all else.

4. Honor God's sovereignty; when you are weak, He is strong.

5. Comprehend the love He has for you so that He can make His home in your heart.

Week 4

ENCOUNTERING HIS PRESENCE

Heidi Baker

*Note: This course is both informational and interactive. One of the objectives of this particular session is to get the group participants to interact with the Holy Spirit. In order to facilitate this interaction, there is an impartation prayer led by Heidi on the DVD.

PRAYER FOCUS: ASK THE HOLY SPIRIT TO GIVE EACH PARTICIPANT *KAIROS* moments in which to experience God in life-changing ways.

FELLOWSHIP AND WELCOME
(10–15 Minutes)

Welcome everyone as they walk in. Be sure to identify any new members who were not at the previous session, and be sure that they receive the appropriate materials—workbook and book.

Encourage everyone to congregate in the meeting place. If it is a classroom setting, make an announcement that it is time to sit down and begin the session. If it is a small group, ensure everyone makes their way to the designated meeting space.

OPENING PRAYER

WORSHIP
(15–20 Minutes)

PRAYER/MINISTRY TIME
(5–15 Minutes)

VIDEO/TEACHING
(25 Minutes)

SCRIPTURE

As God's co-workers we urge you not to receive God's grace in vain. For he says, "In the time of my favor I heard you, and in the day of salvation I helped you." I tell you, now is the time of God's favor, now is the day of salvation (2 Corinthians 6:1-2).

SUMMARY

Did you know there are *kairos* moments when you can experience the Presence of God—life-shattering, life-transitioning moments? That's what we need! We need God to break in and change everything. We need to be in season with the Spirit in that place where God speaks to us like He spoke to Mary through the angel, saying, "You're going to carry a child." And Mary said, "I can't. I'm a virgin." The answer: "I can. I'm God." All you have to say is, "Yes, God, use me."

To encounter His Presence in this way is a lifestyle—a lifestyle of drawing away with God. It's not a stressed-out, "Oh, I hope God shows up!" kind of lifestyle. No, you *know* God will show up because you live with Him. You live in His Presence, and when you live in His Presence God takes your little bitty heart and He breaks it wide open—and you find yourself living in radical compassion. You put the clock, the watch, behind your back and you say, "Yes, Lord," and God does the miraculous! We're just all little tiny people on a little tiny planet, but when we learn to live in the Presence, to live in the embrace of God, everything changes. Absolutely everything changes.

INTERACTIVE QUESTIONS
(25–30 Minutes)

1. The Bible speaks often of *kairos* time. Read Second Corinthians 6:1-2. As you reflect on this passage, ask yourself what it reveals to you about the meaning of *kairos* time.

2. What are your thoughts on taking up a lifestyle of desperation such as Heidi describes? How desperate do you want to be?

3. The issue of surrender is a difficult one for most people. What's getting in the way of your complete surrender to God? Find at least one person in the Bible who had difficulty surrendering to God and reflect on their story.

4. Reflect on the nature of miracles as found in the Gospel of Mark, and identify two or three types of miracles. How do you explain the relationship between miracles and faith?

5. Miracles that seem to us to be outside God's divine laws of nature, such as turning water into wine, may in fact be consistent with aspects of God's nature we are simply not familiar with. What are your thoughts on this statement?

ACTIVATION: UNDERSTANDING KAIROS MOMENTS

Group Activation

We encounter God's presence in the fullness of His time—in *kairos* moments. Ask participants to take a few minutes to search the Scriptures for instances of God's *kairos* time. When everyone has at least a few scriptures, have the group identify the meaning of *kairos* in each scripture. Mark 1:14-15 is an example of where the word *kairos* has a specific meaning. It speaks of a time that demands transformation.

Individual Activation

Search the Bible for instances of God's *kairos* time. Then spend time with the Lord, asking Him to show you how you might take what He teaches you about *kairos* time from Scripture and apply it to the season you are currently in as it relates to the culture around you.

PLANS FOR THE NEXT WEEK
(2 Minutes)

Encourage group members to stay up to date with their daily exercises in the *Living from the Presence Interactive Manual.*

CLOSE IN PRAYER

Week

4

Video Listening Guide:
ENCOUNTERING HIS PRESENCE

Heidi Baker

TO ENCOUNTER HIS PRESENCE IN THIS WAY IS A LIFESTYLE—A LIFESTYLE OF drawing away with God. To live in His embrace changes everything.

There are *kairos* moments when you can experience the Presence of God that are life-shattering and life-transitioning moments. Learn to recognize them.

HOW TO ENCOUNTER HIS PRESENCE

1. Say "yes" to living in His glory and favor where compassion rules your heart.

2. Become radically yielded to God so that there is no room for "no" in your life.

3. Get desperate enough to become dependent on His miracles.

4. Live free and holy, allowing God to change your heart so that you can delight in doing His will.

5. Encounter His Presence in the miraculous and worship Him!

Week

5

CLINGING TO HIS PRESENCE IN CHALLENGES

Heidi Baker

PRAYER FOCUS: ASK THE HOLY SPIRIT TO INCREASE THE ABILITY OF EACH participant to experience God's embrace in the midst of life's challenges.

FELLOWSHIP AND WELCOME
(10–15 Minutes)

Welcome everyone as they walk in. Be sure to identify any new members who were not at the previous session, and be sure that they receive the appropriate materials—workbook and book.

Encourage everyone to congregate in the meeting place. If it is a classroom setting, make an announcement that it is time to sit down and begin the session. If it is a small group, ensure everyone makes their way to the designated meeting space.

OPENING PRAYER

WORSHIP
(15–20 Minutes)

PRAYER/MINISTRY TIME
(5–15 Minutes)

VIDEO/TEACHING
(20 Minutes)

SCRIPTURE

With your whole being you embrace God setting things right, and then you say it, right out loud: "God has set everything right between him and me!" Scripture reassures us, "No one who trusts God like this—heart and soul—will ever regret it" (Romans 10:10-11 MSG).

SUMMARY

Living in God's Presence is all about being in His embrace. We want to live inside God's embrace, to feel His arms around us, His love surrounding us. When you are in God's embrace, you are where He is and He is where you are. My absolute favorite chapter on God's presence is Exodus 33. There are many beautiful aspects of His character we can learn from this chapter. Like Moses, we want God to be pleased with us so He will teach us His ways and His will for our lives. We want to feel favored by God—ultimately feeling His embrace and sensing Him saying, "Look at My team. Look at My family. I want to hug them. I want to go with them on their life journey and give them rest when they are weary." That's living in God's embrace! When we are in His embrace, life's challenges give way to His mighty Presence.

INTERACTIVE QUESTIONS
(25–30 Minutes)

1. Heidi highlights three aspects of God's character from Exodus 33. What is your take-away from these passages?

   [Moses said,] *"If you are pleased with me, teach me your ways so I may know you and continue to find favor with you...."*

   The Lord replied, "My Presence will go with you, and I will give you rest."

   Then Moses said to him, "If your Presence does not go with us, do not send us up from here."

   ...And the Lord said, "I will cause all my goodness to pass in front of you, and I will proclaim my name, the Lord, in your presence" (Exodus 33:13–15,19).

   _____

   _____

   _____

   _____

   _____

2. Are you a Mary or a Martha? Are you living in the moment or constantly distracted? Explain.

   _____

   _____

   _____

   _____

   _____

3. How do you answer the question, "What distinguishes you from other people on the face of the earth?"

4. What does it mean to be a "hard sell" like Pharaoh?

5. Using examples from Scripture other than the prodigal son, how does Father God respond to wayward hearts?

6. Search the New Testament and find at least two places where Jesus brings the spiritually dead to life. How did He accomplish this?

ACTIVATION: THE BEAUTIFUL ASPECTS OF GOD'S CHARACTER

Read Exodus 33, looking for the beautiful aspects of God's character. When Moses petitions the Lord in prayer on behalf of the people of Israel, God responds graciously. Notice in verse 12 that Moses is not willing to settle for an angel to accompany them; he desires the very Presence of God, and God does not deny him.

Group Activation

Have everyone read Exodus 33, making note of the beautiful aspects of God's character found in this portion of Scripture. Invite people to share, with a focus on the desire of Moses for God's Presence.

Individual Activation

Read Exodus 33, making note of the beautiful aspects of God's character found in this chapter. Reflect on Moses' desire for the Presence of God versus an angel. Based on your knowledge of Scripture, did Moses set a precedent for the way in which we are to relate to God?

Goal

Encourage participants to examine the way in which they relate to God in light of His character.

PLANS FOR THE NEXT WEEK
(2 Minutes)

Encourage group members to stay up to date with their daily exercises in the *Living from the Presence Interactive Manual.*

CLOSE IN PRAYER

Week

5

Video Listening Guide:
CLINGING TO HIS PRESENCE
IN CHALLENGES

Heidi Baker

LIVING IN GOD'S PRESENCE IS ALL ABOUT BEING IN HIS EMBRACE. WE WANT TO live inside God's embrace, to feel His arms around us, His love surrounding us.

When you are in God's embrace, you are where He is and He is where you are.

HOW TO CLING TO HIS PRESENCE IN CHALLENGES

1.   Live in the moment with God, absorbed by Him, connected with Him.

2.   Build a strong personal relationship with God, like Moses did.

3.   Let the goodness of God soften your heart so that you can see as He sees.

4.   Know that God will always meet you with a Father's embrace.

5.   Become completely pliable, completely obedient, completely in love and allow yourself to be used.

Week
6

PRACTICAL KEYS TO EXPERIENCING HIS PRESENCE

Heidi Baker

PRAYER FOCUS: ASK THE HOLY SPIRIT TO HELP EVERY PARTICIPANT IDENTIFY what the presence of God looks like in their lives.

FELLOWSHIP AND WELCOME
(10–15 Minutes)

Welcome everyone as they walk in. Be sure to identify any new members who were not at the previous session, and be sure that they receive the appropriate materials—workbook and book.

Encourage everyone to congregate in the meeting place. If it is a classroom setting, make an announcement that it is time to sit down and begin the session. If it is a small group, ensure everyone makes their way to the designated meeting space.

OPENING PRAYER

WORSHIP
(10–15 Minutes)

PRAYER/MINISTRY TIME
(5–15 Minutes)

VIDEO/TEACHING
(20 Minutes)

SCRIPTURE

And my God will meet all your needs according to the riches of his glory in Christ Jesus (Philippians 4:19).

SUMMARY

What does the Presence look like? For me, one day the Presence looked like a broken machine gun. Other days it looks like the glory cloud. Glory looks like something; Presence looks like something. In Exodus 33, the Presence looks like a combination of God's Word, a promise, an angel, power to destroy the enemy, prosperity. The Lord told Moses to leave, to get up and get out of that place and go to his place of promise. *"Leave this place, you and the people you brought up out of Egypt, and go up to a land I promised on oath"* (Exod. 33:1).

For me, that land God promised me on oath is Mozambique. Maybe my twenty-two years there should have been easy. Maybe the Presence of God just wafts in at all times in such a way that I never feel the stress. Well, that hasn't been the case—but no matter the stress, His peace is so deep and so connected to Him that each challenge is defeated even before I face it. Moses has a promise from God. If you want to know about the Presence, you have to know about your promise. When I knew I had to face the angry crowd and the machine guns, there was something inside supporting me. I had no earthly weapon. The weapon I walked in with was our big God. I knew His Presence would manifest in the perfect way for the situation because He promised me. When you live in His Presence, promises come to pass. God never retracts His promises. All you need to do is accept the promises in faith.

INTERACTIVE QUESTIONS
(25–30 Minutes)

1. What do you think about living in God's Presence to such a great extent that His power is present to make the enemy tremble? What is Heidi talking about with this statement?

2. How would you explain to someone what it means to "get out there in the Presence of Jesus"?

3. Heidi talks about "unpacking God" so that He can overshadow you with His Presence. What is she talking about? As you reflect on this question, think about Mary, the mother of Jesus. She had obviously "unpacked" God because of the way in which she responded when His Presence overshadowed her. What do the ways in which you have responded to God indicate about how you unpack your heavenly Father?

4. When Heidi talks about "living lean" in the Presence of God, she's not talking about losing weight, although she could be. What does it mean to "live lean"?

5. When God uses the term "stiff-necked," it's not meant to be endearing. What implications does the term "stiff-necked" as God uses it in Scripture have for you?

6. In Romans, Paul talks about exchanging the glory of immortal God for things of no value. What does it mean to exchange the glory of God? Has any of this kind of exchange taken place in your life?

_____

_____

_____

_____

7. What does promise have to do with experiencing His Presence?

_____

_____

_____

_____

ACTIVATION: EXPERIENCING HIS PRESENCE BECAUSE OF HIS PROMISES

Group Activation

As a way of better understanding practical keys to experiencing God's Presence, invite group members to reflect silently on those times when they have experienced God's Presence because of His promises. Allow a time for everyone to share their experiences.

Individual Activation

As a way of better understanding practical keys to experiencing God's Presence, reflect on those times when you have experienced God's Presence because of His promises. Make note of those instances and hold them in your heart for those times in the future when you'll need to remember His promises when in need of His Presence.

PLANS FOR THE NEXT WEEK
(2 Minutes)

Encourage group members to stay up to date with their daily exercises in the *Living from the Presence Interactive Manual.*

CLOSE IN PRAYER

Week

6

Video Listening Guide:
PRACTICAL KEYS TO EXPERIENCING HIS PRESENCE

Heidi Baker

THE WEAPON YOU WANT WALK TO IN WITH IS OUR BIG GOD, KNOWING THAT His Presence will manifest in the perfect way for the situation because He promised us.

When you live in His Presence, promises come to pass. God never retracts His promises. All you need to do is accept the promises in faith.

PRACTICAL KEYS TO EXPERIENCING HIS PRESENCE

1. Be strong and courageous in His Presence.

2. Believe in Him so that when you get into situations that require faith, you can trust that He will show up.

3. Live outside the box so that He can overshadow you with His Presence. There are no limits to what God can do.

4. Learn to live lean as a yielded lover, rejecting anything that doesn't bring Him glory.

5. Cast off idolatry—anything and everything that is separating you from God and His Presence.

YOUR IDENTITY IN HIS PRESENCE

Heidi Baker

PRAYER FOCUS: ASK THE LORD TO STIR UP A HOLY HUNGER IN EACH PERSON'S heart to experience His Presence in order to live in His Presence so that they may carry His Presence into the world with compassion and humility.

FELLOWSHIP AND WELCOME
(10–15 Minutes)

Welcome everyone as they walk in. Be sure to identify any new members who were not at the previous session, and be sure that they receive the appropriate materials—workbook and book.

Encourage everyone to congregate in the meeting place. If it is a classroom setting, make an announcement that it is time to sit down and begin the session. If it is a small group, ensure everyone makes their way to the designated meeting space.

OPENING PRAYER

WORSHIP
(15–20 Minutes)

Feel free to shorten the worship time at the beginning of the session, as the activation exercise will consist of a worship segment.

PRAYER/MINISTRY TIME
(5–15 Minutes)

VIDEO/TEACHING
(20 Minutes)

SCRIPTURE

For we do not have a high priest who is unable to empathize with our weaknesses, but we have one who has been tempted in every way, just as we are—yet he did not sin (Hebrews 4:15).

SUMMARY

During this time of listening and watching and showing and telling, I believe that God is creating a holy hunger to not just *experience* His Presence, but to *live* in His manifest Presence;

and not just to *live* in His manifest Presence, but to *carry* His manifest Presence, which is compassion and mercy and glory and kindness and meekness. We are to carry it into our homes, into our schools and the workplace, into the malls, the streets, the famine zones, and out among the unreached people groups of the world.

Jesus is the point of our existence. *"She will give birth to a son, and you are to give him the name Jesus, because he will save his people from their sins"* (Matt. 1:21). Before He was born, Jesus' purpose was to save us from ourselves—our sinful nature. Without Jesus we are lost, unable to be reunited with the heavenly Father. With Him we have purpose—His purpose. In Him we find identity—knowing who we are in Christ. There are many benefits of being saved. One of the most important is being connected to Jesus in our everyday lives. Jesus is the basis for the Kingdom-effect on earth.

Jesus was humble, always pointing to His heavenly Father, teaching people how to get closer to the Lord so they could live the abundant life promised to them. When asked by an expert in the law which of the commandments was the greatest, *"Jesus replied: 'Love the Lord your God with all your heart and with all your soul and with all your mind'"* (Matt. 22:37). What does it mean to love the Lord your God with all your heart and mind and soul and strength? Think about that. Is it possible for us to love with *all* of our heart, soul, and mind? Probably not. We need Holy Spirit to help us understand what our spirits are capable of. Holy Spirit will do that for you. All you have to do is ask.

INTERACTIVE QUESTIONS
(25–30 Minutes)

1. The compassion of God in Jesus is displayed throughout the gospels. Find some examples of God's compassion in Scripture, in either the New or Old Testament. Then, identify examples of God's compassion in your life.

2. How can you stand beside Jesus in intercession to help build His church? Where in Scripture do we find the importance of intercession?

3. What does it mean to be "washed clean" so that others can see Jesus through us?

4. Heidi talks about becoming "humbly strong" like the humble Bridegroom. Identify some of the ways in which Jesus demonstrates humility for us in the Scriptures. How have you demonstrated His humility in your own environment?

5. Heidi says that the only way we can live in the Presence is if we realize and recognize the love of the Father for His Son. How has God demonstrated this love? How do you think He wants you to demonstrate it?

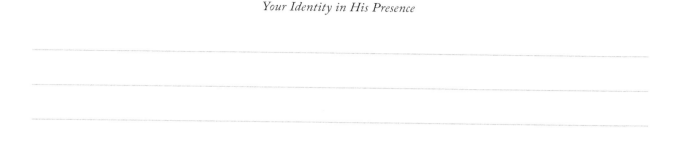

ACTIVATION: UNDERSTANDING THE COMPASSION OF GOD

Compassion is a very significant aspect of Jesus' character. And as Jesus is an exact representation of the Father, then it is also a significant aspect of God's character.

Group Activation

Have participants reflect on God's compassion in their own lives, asking them to think about how God's compassion toward them has made them more compassionate. Invite them to share as they feel led.

Individual Activation

Reflect on God's compassion in your life. How has God's compassion toward you made you more compassionate?

PLANS FOR THE NEXT WEEK
(2 Minutes)

Let participants know that next week is the final week of the study.

CLOSE IN PRAYER

Week
7

Video Listening Guide:
YOUR IDENTITY IN
HIS PRESENCE

Heidi Baker

WITHOUT JESUS WE ARE LOST, UNABLE TO BE REUNITED WITH THE HEAVENLY Father. With Him we have purpose—His purpose.

In Him we find identity, knowing who we are in Christ.

FINDING YOUR IDENTITY IN HIS PRESENCE

1. Always desire more of Jesus, our perfect human companion, full of compassion.

2. Enter the Holy Place with confidence in Jesus our great intercessor. This is part of your inheritance and identity.

3. Learn to be His servant in all that you do so that others can see Jesus in you.

4. Stay strong in your faith and humble in your attitude. A humble spirit grows the closer you get to Jesus, the humble Bridegroom.

5. Recognize the love of the Father for His Son and learn to love like Jesus.

Week
8

TO BE SATURATED BY GOD'S PRESENCE

Heidi Baker

*Note: Like Session 4, one of the objectives of Session 8 is to get group participants to interact with the Holy Spirit. In order to facilitate this interaction, there is an impartation prayer led by Heidi on the DVD.

PRAYER FOCUS: ASK THE LORD TO GIVE EVERY PARTICIPANT A REVELATION OF His ways in which they can be saturated in God's Presence as a lifestyle.

FELLOWSHIP AND WELCOME
(10–15 Minutes)

Welcome everyone as they walk in. Be sure to identify any new members who were not at the previous session, and be sure that they receive the appropriate materials—workbook and book.

Encourage everyone to congregate in the meeting place. If it is a classroom setting, make an announcement that it is time to sit down and begin the session. If it is a small group, ensure everyone makes their way to the designated meeting space.

OPENING PRAYER

WORSHIP
(15–20 Minutes)

PRAYER/MINISTRY TIME
(10 minutes)

VIDEO/TEACHING
(20 Minutes)

SCRIPTURE

Whatever you have learned or received or heard from me, or seen in me—put it into practice. And the God of peace will be with you (Philippians 4:9).

SUMMARY

It is important for believers to have a dedicated, yielded time in the secret place. This is not a time when you're looking at your watch, trying to figure out what to do next. This is when you say to the Lord, "I must encounter Your Presence! I yield my mind, heart, emotions—my entire life to connect to You, the living God." This is the first step. When you take it, you will submerge into His Presence.

In Exodus 33, we find Moses in this place of utter yieldness.

> *As Moses went into the tent, the pillar of cloud would come down and stay at the entrance, while the Lord spoke with Moses. Whenever the people saw the pillar of cloud standing at the entrance to the tent, they all stood and worshiped, each at the entrance to their tent.* **The Lord would speak to Moses face to face, as one speaks to a friend** (Exodus 33:9–11).

Did you catch that: "face to face, as one speaks to a friend"? Isn't that the best? Do you want a heart-to-heart conversation with God? Just yield completely to Him. Lay everything down and enter into His marvelous, holy Presence. There is nothing better this side of Heaven.

Living from His Presence is a lifestyle that requires a lifestyle of learning. God is a willing teacher. Place your hand in His hand and learn from Him. Jesus said, *"Take my yoke upon you and learn from me, for I am gentle and humble in heart, and you will find rest for your souls"* (Matt. 11:29).

INTERACTIVE QUESTIONS
(25–30 Minutes)

1. In Day 1, Heidi speaks of "obedience to the Gentle Master." Jesus is our kind, tender Master—our sympathetic, benevolent, compassionate King. Why do you think it is so difficult for us to yield to Jesus when His nature is so loving and welcoming?

2. God is calling you daily to press in to His Presence, and then press in more. Why? Why do you think God desires your presence?

3. Ananias, a disciple of Jesus in Damascus, was just a little piece of a big picture—a catalyst for God's Kingdom (see Acts 9:10–19). When God came with instructions to pray for Saul, Ananias was so frightened by what he had heard about Saul that he really didn't want to do what God was asking of him, yet he obeyed. The result has impacted the world for Christ and His Kingdom in ways that Ananias never could have imagined. One would be led to believe that this seemingly insignificant disciple was living from God's Presence. How else would he have been able to overcome fear for his very life? Remember, Saul was having Christians killed. What has God called you to do that has made you fearful? Has your relationship with Him enabled you to overcome your fear, or not?

4. It sounds so marvelous when Heidi says things like "living fully alive in His glory." How does this reconcile with the reality of holding a horribly disfigured child in your arms in a dirty street?

5. What does Heidi means when she says, "He deals with His children differently than He deals with the rest of the world"?

_____

_____

_____

_____

_____

ACTIVATION: PRESSING IN FOR MORE

Group Activation

In this session, Heidi focuses on five ways in which we can be saturated in God's Presence—obedience, pressing in, being a catalyst for the Kingdom, living fully alive in His glory, and understanding our inheritance as believers. Ask group members which one or ones of these five they find easiest to do, and which one(s) are hardest? Invite people to share as they feel led.

Individual Activation

In this session, Heidi focuses on five ways in which we can be saturated in God's Presence—obedience, pressing in, being a catalyst for the Kingdom, living fully alive in His glory, and understanding our inheritance as believers. Which one or ones of these five do you find easiest to do, and which one(s) are hardest? How might you tackle the harder ones?

PLANS FOR THE NEXT WEEK
(2 Minutes)

Let participants know that either this is the final week of the study or that you will be having some type of social activity on the following week—or at a specified future date.

CLOSE IN PRAYER

Pray that the group would truly be able to strengthen themselves in the Lord as they continue to daily walk out the tools that have been presented throughout the course.

Week
8

Video Listening Guide:
TO BE SATURATED BY GOD'S PRESENCE

Heidi Baker

Interact with the Holy Spirit through the impartation prayer led by Heidi.

IT IS IMPORTANT TO HAVE A DEDICATED, YIELDED TIME IN THE SECRET PLACE. This is when you say to the Lord, "I must encounter Your Presence! I yield my mind, heart, emotions, my entire life to connect to You, the living God."

Living from His Presence requires a lifestyle of learning. God is a willing teacher. Place your hand in His hand and learn from Him.

HOW TO BE SATURATED BY GOD'S PRESENCE

1. Be obedient to His voice even when your flesh is weak.

2. Do what He gives you to do, and then press in to Him.

3. Be a catalyst for the Kingdom, understanding that you are just a little piece of the whole.

4. Come fully alive in His glory no matter the circumstances.

5. Know that you are indeed a beloved child of God called to a higher standard, a different way of life, and a greater hope.

ABOUT HEIDI AND ROLLAND BAKER

ROLLAND AND HEIDI BAKER, FOUNDERS AND DIRECTORS OF IRIS GLOBAL, HAVE served as missionaries for more than 35 years to the world's poorest people. Heidi earned her PhD degree at King's College, University of London, where the Bakers planted a thriving church for the homeless. Rolland has his Doctor of Ministry (D. Min.) from United Theological Seminary located in Dayton, Ohio. They have lived and ministered for the last 21 years in Mozambique. They also travel internationally, teaching about "passion and compassion" in the ministry of the Gospel. They have written several books, including *Always Enough, Expecting Miracles, Compelled by Love, Birthing the Miraculous, Reckless Devotion* and *Training for Harvest*.

Notes

FREE E-BOOKS?
YES, PLEASE!

Get **FREE** and deeply-discounted **Christian books** for your **e-reader** delivered to your inbox **every week!**

IT'S SIMPLE!

VISIT lovetoreadclub.com

SUBSCRIBE by entering your email address

RECEIVE free and discounted e-book offers and inspiring articles delivered to your inbox every week!

Unsubscribe at any time.

SUBSCRIBE NOW!

LOVE TO READ CLUB

visit **LOVETOREADCLUB.COM** ▶